ASSASSINATIONS IN THE SKY

Edward Jay Epstein Investigates

By Edward Jay Epstein

A Short-form Book

Published by FastTrack Press/ EJE Publications, Ltd.
New York, New York

Copyright © by EJE Publication 2011, 2013 All Rights Reserved
Volume II in the series: *Edward Jay Epstein Investigates*
Revised: March15,2020

ALSO BY EDWARD JAY EPSTEIN

Inquest: The Warren Commission and the Establishment of Truth

Counterplot: Garrison vs. the United States

News from Nowhere: Television and the News

Between Fact and Fiction: The Problem of Journalism

Agency of Fear: Opiates and Political Power in America

Legend: The Secret World of Lee Harvey Oswald

The Rise and Fall of Diamonds

Who Owns the Corporation?

Deception: The Invisible War Between the KGB and the CIA

The Assassination Chronicles

Dossier: The Secret History of Armand Hammer

The Big Picture: Money and Power in

Hollywood

The Hollywood Economist

Annals of Unsolved Crime

How America Lost its Secrets: Edward Snowden, the Man and the Theft

James Jesus Angleton: Was He Right?

CONTENT

Preface
Chapter 1   Killing Zia
Chapter 2   The Death of Dag Hammarskjöld
Chapter 3   The Killing of Enrico Mattei
Chapter 4   Vanishing Lin Baio

Appendix A   Political Plane Crashes

PREFACE

If a plane is made to disappear in the ocean, explode over a remote area or be consumed in a fire, all evidence of the true cause of the crash may be lost. Such assassinations in the sky come close to being the perfect murder. Investigators may not even be able to resolve the question whether the cause was pilot's error, weather, mechical failure or sabotage. Even when possibly incriminating evidence is recovered from the wreckage, it is often ambiguous. Consider, for example, the crash over the ocean of TWA flight 800 on July 17, 1996, that resulted in the death of 230 people. Much of the wreckage was recovered from the ocean and, from it, the FBI lab in Washington, D.C identified traces of three different explosives, RDX, PETN, and nitroglycerin on pieces of the plate. All three chemicals are used in bomb making, and they could be interpreted as signatures of sabotage. They also could have been the result of prior security tests—airlines use live explosives on planes to test their sniffer dogs and other detection equipment—or of the transportation of troops during the 1991 Gulf War. When this discovery was considered in the context of other evidence, the National Transport Safety Board concluded that the latter had occurred and ruled that the crash was the result of an accidental gas leak, not sabotage.

I first realized how contentious and complex aircraft investigations could be when I went to Pakistan to investigate the plane crash that killed General Zia-ul-Haq, the military dictator of that country, in 1988. Even with sophisticated forensic analysis by the plane's manufacturer, it could not be determined why the plane had crashed, because crucial evidence was missing: the government had disposed of the bodies of the pilots before they could be medically examined. It was this case that excited my interest in sky assassinations.

To be sure, there are unsolved mysteries that defy a solution. Malaysia Airlines Flight 370, on a routine flight from Kuala Lumpur in Malaysia to Beijing, China, literally vanished in mid air in the early morning of March 8, 2014. At 1:19 am, just as the Boeing 777-200, with 239 people aboard, was leaving Malaysia's airspace over the South China Sea, someone in the cockpit said "Good night Malaysian three-seven-zero," moments later the transponders in the cockpit, which identify the plane to air traffic controllers, went off. Nor was the plane's Aircraft Communications Addressing and Reporting System (ACARS), which sends data about every 30 minutes to Malaysian Airlines and Boeing, heard from again. Military radar in Malaysia and Thailand detected an unidentified airplane flying back into Malaysian airspace and the Gulf of Thailand but that aircraft, after changing its altitude at least twice, then disappeared from the radar. The only evidence that Flight 370 was still intact was weak pings detected by a satellite over the Indian Ocean for the next seven hour. The searched focused on an area in the Indian Ocean about 1200 miles from Australia, but, despite a month long search by an International task force of ships, planes, and satellites, no debris from the plane was found.

The real mystery was what had caused Flight 370 to so radically divert its course. The *New York Times* reported, base on information provided from Boeing, that sometime, prior to 1:07 a.m. when the last transmission of data was made by ACARS, someone in the cockpit had keyed into the flight management computer a string of digits that would divert the flight. If so, it would suggest a premeditated diversion and the possibility that the plane had been commandeered. However, CNN, citing a source in the Malaysian investigation, reported that the ACARS did not show any such diversion. If so, it is possible that a series of accidents led to the plane's diversion and silence. Although some debris from the place was found, the plane's back box was never found. Without it, the mystery cannot be solved.

This book investigates four plane crashes that changed history: the crash of President Zia and his top generals in Pakistan, the crash of UN Secretary General Dag Hammarskjöld in East Africa, the crash of ENI chairman Enrico Mattei in Italy and the crash of Marshal Lin Baio in China.

Chapter 1

KILLING ZIA

The death of President Muhammad Zia-ul-Haq of Pakistan and his top deputies, in August 1988 altered the face of the country's politics in Pakistan in a way in which no simple coup d'état could have done. Pakistan is the only country named after an acronym: "P" stands for Punjab, "A" for Afghanistan, and the "K" for Kashmiri. It once reflected the dream of a transAsia Islamic state; only the "P" actually became part of Pakistan when it was carved out of British India in 1947 as a haven for Muslims. General Zia was mindful of this dream when he organized a military coup in 1977 and seized power. Zia moved almost immediately to placate the mullahs in his country by pursuing a policy of "Islamization" and reinstating the law of the Koran. In an extraordinary balancing act, he also strove to build an ultra-modern military machine, complete with nuclear arms, and also to use his intelligence service, the ISI, to wage war against the Soviet occupiers of Afghanistan and the Indian army in Kashmiri. This great game, and his regime, came to an abrupt end on August 17, 1988.
I went to Pakistan in the winter of 1989 on a *Vanity Fair* assignment to investigate Zia's death. Soon after I arrived in Islamabad, I found that the Pakistani officials I had made arrangements to interview were no longer available to me, either on or off the record. One aide to the foreign minister said that the subject of the "tragic accident," as he termed the plane crash that had killed general Zia, was now off limits. Since the Pakistan government was stonewalling, I turned for assistance to the only other source I could find:

the children of the generals killed in the crash. My assumption that they had a motive to discover what was behind the death of their fathers proved correct. A number of these young men, including the sons of General Zia and General Akhtar Abdur Rahman (who for ten years had headed Pakistan's equivalent of the CIA, the InterServices Intelligence agency, or ISI), most of whom were in their mid-twenties, not only proved enormously eager to help but, through the medium of their fathers' military aides, had access to key officials, including the airport security officers at the control towers who had actually taped the final conversation from Zia's plane, and the medical officers who had superintended the disposal of the bodies after the crash. With their help, I was able to gradually piece together the story.

On August 17, General Zia boarded Pak One, an Americanbuilt Hercules C-130 transport plane, at the military air base outside of Bahawalpur, Pakistan. He had reluctantly gone to Bahawalpur that morning, on his first trip aboard Pak One since May 29, to witness a demonstration of the new American Abrams tank. The plane took off at 3:46 p.m., precisely on schedule for the trip back to the capital city of Islamabad. Seated next to Zia in the air-conditioned VIP capsule was General Akhtar Abdur Rahman, then Chairman of the Joint Chiefs of Staff and, after Zia, the second most powerful man in Pakistan. Among the other passengers were General Mohamed Afzal, Zia's chief of the General Staff; eight other Pakistan generals; Zia's top aides; and two American guests: Ambassador Arnold L. Raphel, and General Herbert M. Wassom, the head of the U.S. military-aid mission to Pakistan.

Shortly after takeoff, only eighteen miles from the airport, on a bright clear day, the giant aircraft lurched up and down three times in the sky, as if were on an invisible roller coaster, and then plunged straight into the desert and exploded in a fireball. All thirty persons on board, including four crew members, were dead. Within hours, army tanks sealed off public buildings and television stations, signifying a change in power. But the mystery remained: What caused the plane to crash?

Since it involved an American-built plane, and the CIA had been partners with Zia in the war against Soviet forces in Afghanistan, the United States obtained permission for U.S. forensic experts to carry out the investigation for Pakistan's board of inquiry. But Pakistan limited the number of U.S. experts to seven Air Force accident investigators and specifically excluded any criminal, counterterrorist, or sabotage experts. The team, headed by Colonel Daniel E. Sowada, issued a 365-page red-bound report, which I obtained from a source at the Pentagon. The team had worked to eliminate what was not possible, following the precept that once the impossible is eliminated, what remains, no matter how improbable, is the truth. First, they ruled out the possibility that the plane had blown up in midair. If it had exploded in this manner, the pieces of the plane, which had different shapes and therefore different resistance to wind, would have been strewn over a wide area—but that had not happened. By reassembling the plane in a giant jigsaw puzzle and scrutinizing with magnifying glasses the edges of each broken piece, they established that the plane was in one piece when it had hit the ground. They thus concluded that structural failure—i.e. the breaking-up of the plane in flight—was not the cause. Next, they eliminated the possibility of a missile attack. If the plane had been hit by a missile, intense heat would have melted the aluminum panels and, as the plane dived, the wind would have left telltale streaks in the molten metal. But there were no streaks on the panels, and no missile part or other ordnance had been found in the area.

They further ruled out the possibility that there was an onboard fire while the plane was in the air since, if there had been one, the passengers would have breathed in soot before they died. Yet, the single autopsy performed, which was on the American general seated in the VIP capsule, showed that there was no soot in his trachea, indicating that he had died before, not after, the fire ignited by the crash.

If it was not a missile or fire, another possibility was power failure. If that had happened, the propellers would not have been turning at their full torque when the plane crashed, which would have affected the way that their blades had broken off and curled on impact. But by examining the degree of curling on each broken propeller blade, the investigators determined that in fact the propellers were spinning at full speed when the plane hit the ground.

Next they turned to the fuel. They ruled out the possibility of contaminated fuel by taking samples of the diesel fuel from the refueling truck, and by analyzing the residues still left in the fuel pumps in the plane, which they determined had been operating normally at the time of the crash. They also ruled out any problem with the electric power on the plane because both electric clocks on board had stopped at the exact moment of impact. The final possibility for a mechanical failure was that the controls became inoperable. But the Hercules C-130 had not one but three redundant control system. The two sets of hydraulic controls were backed up, in case of leaks of fluid in both of them, by a mechanical system of cables. If any one of them worked, the pilots would have been able to fly the plane. By comparing the position of the controls with the mechanisms in the hydraulic valves and the stabilizers in the tail of the plane (which are moved through this system when the pilot moves the steering wheel), they established that the control system was working when the plane crashed. This was confirmed by a computer simulation of the flight performed by Lockheed, the builder of the C-130. They also ruled out the possibility that the controls had temporarily jammed by a microscopic examination of the mechanical parts to see if there were any signs of jamming or binding.

That left the possibility of pilot error. But the crash had occurred after a routine and safe takeoff in perfectly clear daytime weather, and the hand-picked pilots were fully experienced with the C-130 and had medical checkups before the flight. Since the plane was not in any critical phase of flight, such as takeoff or landing, where poor judgment on the part of the pilots could have resulted in the mishap, the investigators ruled out pilot error as a possible cause. Since they precluded both a mechanical failure and pilot error, a conclusion of assassination was all but inescapable.

Based on this investigation, Pakistan's board of inquiry concluded that the cause of the crash of Pak One was a criminal act "leading to the loss of control of the aircraft." It suggested that the pilots must have been incapacitated, but this was as far as it could go, since there was no black box or cockpit recorder on Pak One and no autopsies had been done on the remains of the pilots.

What had happened to the pilots during the final minutes of the flight? When I went to Pakistan in February 1989, I attempted to answer that question by finding other planes in the area that might have intercepted radio reports from Pak One. There were three other planes in the area tuned to the same frequency for communications—a turbojet carrying General Aslam Beg, the Army's vice chief of staff, which was waiting on the runway at Bahawalpur airport to take off next; Pak 379, which was the backup C-130 in case anything went wrong to delay Pak One; and a Cessna security plane that took off before Pak One to scout for terrorists. With the assistance of the families of the military leaders killed in the crash, I managed to locate the pilots of these planes—all of whom were well acquainted with the flight crew of Pak One and its procedures— who could listen to the conversation between Pak One and the control tower in Bahawalpur. They independently described the same sequence of events. First, Pak One reported its estimated time of arrival in the capital. Then, when the control tower asked its position, it failed to respond. At the same time Pak 379 was trying unsuccessfully to get in touch with Pak One to verify its arrival time. All they heard from Pak One was "Stand by," but no message followed. When this silence persisted, the control tower became progressively more frantic in its efforts to contact Zia's pilot, Wing Commander Mash'hood. Three or four minutes passed. Then, a faint voice in Pak One called out "Mash'hood, Mash'hood." One of the pilots overhearing this conversation recognized the voice. It was Zia's military secretary, Brigadier Najib Ahmed, who apparently, from the low volume of his voice, was in the back of the flight deck (where a door connected to the VIP capsule). If the radio was switched on and was picking up background sounds, it was the next-best thing to a cockpit flight recorder. Under these circumstances, the long silence between "Stand by" and the faint calls to Mash'hood, like the dog that didn't bark, was the relevant fact. Why wouldn't Mash'hood or any of the three other members of the flight crew have spoken if they were in trouble? The pilots aboard the other planes, who were fully familiar with Mash'hood, and the procedures he was trained in, explained that if Pak One's crew was conscious and in trouble, they would not in any circumstances have remained silent for this period of time. If there had been difficulties with controls, Mash'hood would have instantly given the emergency "Mayday" signal so help would be dispatched to the scene. Even if he had for some reason chosen not to communicate with the control tower, he would have been heard shouting orders to his crew to prepare for an emergency landing. And if there had been an attempt at a hijacking in the cockpit or a scuffle between the pilots, it would also be overheard. In retrospect, the pilots of the other aircraft had only one explanation for the prolonged silence: Mash'hood and the other pilots were unconscious while the thumb switch that operated the microphone had been kept opened by the clenched hand of a pilot.

The account of the eyewitnesses at the crash site dovetailed with the radio silence. They had seen the plane slowly pitching up and down. According to a C-130 expert to whom I spoke at Lockheed, a C-130 characteristically goes into a pattern known as a "phugoid" when no pilot is flying it. First, the unattended plane dives toward the ground then the mechanism in the tail automatically overcorrects for this downward motion, causing the plane to head momentarily upward. This pattern would continue, each swing becoming more pronounced until the plane crashed. Analyzing the weight on the plane, and how it had been loaded, this expert calculated that the plane would have made three roller-coaster turns before crashing, which is exactly what the witnesses had reported. He concluded from this pattern that had the pilots been conscious, they would have corrected the "phugoid"—or at least, would have made an effort, which would have been reflected in the settings of the controls. Since this had not happened, only one possibility remained: the pilots were paralyzed, unconscious, or dead.

Meanwhile, an analysis of chemicals found in the plane's wreckage, performed by the laboratory of the Bureau of Alcohol, Firearms, and Tobacco in Washington, D.C., found foreign traces of pentaerythritol tertranitrate (PNET), a secondary high explosive commonly used by saboteurs as a detonator, as well as antimony and sulfur, which, in the compound antimony sulfide, is used in fuses to set off such a device. Using these same chemicals, Pakistan ordnance experts reconstructed a low-level explosive detonator that could have been used to burst a flask the size of a soda can. These tests showed that it was possible that such a device could have been used to dispense an odorless poison gas that incapacitated the pilots.

Indeed, the ATF lab also found phosphorous residue in the cockpit, which could have come from poison gas.

The problem in pursuing this lead was that no medical examinations or autopsies were performed on the bodies of the pilots and other members of the flight crew. Doctors at the military hospital in Bahawalpur reported that parts of the victims' bodies had been brought there in plastic body bags from the crash site on the night of August 17, and stored there, so that autopsies could be performed by a team of American and Pakistani pathologists. But before the pathologists had arrived, the hospital received orders to return these plastic bags to the coffins for burial. The commanding officer ordered the medical preparations to cease and the bodies to be turned over for immediate burial. The official explanation given in the report is that Islamic law requires burial within twenty-four hours. But this could not have been the real reason, since the bodies were not returned to their families for burial until two days after the crash, as relatives confirmed to me. Nor were the families ever asked permission for autopsy examinations. And, as I learned from a doctor for the Pakistan Air Force, Islamic law notwithstanding, autopsies are routinely done on pilots in cases of air crashes. This intervention made it impossible to determine whether a nerve gas or other toxic agent had paralyzed the crew.

These orders to literally bury the evidence came directly from the Army, which was now under the authority of General Beg, who, after having his turbojet pilot circle over the burning wreckage of Pak One, flew immediately back to Islamabad, to assume command. For their part, Pakistani military authorities concentrated their investigation on the possibility that Shiite fanatics were responsible for the crash. The copilot of Pak One, Wing Commander Sajid, was a Shiite (as are more than ten percent of Pakistan's Muslims), as was one of the pilots of the backup C-130. This pilot, though he protested his innocence, was kept in custody for more than two months and roughly interrogated about whether Wing Commander Sajid had discussed a suicide mission. Finally, the Army abandoned this effort after the Air Force demonstrated that it would have been physically impossible for the copilot alone to have caused a C-130 to crash in the way it did.

The government then appointed a commission headed by Justice Shafiur Rehman, a well-respected judge on the Supreme Court, to establish the cause of the crash. Five years later, in 1993, it issued a secret report concluding that the Army had so effectively obstructed the investigation that the perpetrators behind the crash could not be brought to justice. The one uncounted casualty of Pak One was thus the truth.

There is, to be sure, an abundance theories based on who had a motive to kill General Zia. Not unlike the plot of Agatha Christie's *Murder on the Orient Express*, in which, if one looked hard enough, everyone aboard the train had a motive for the murder, many parties, with the means to sabotage a plane, had a motive to eliminate Zia.

First, there is the CIA. According to this theory, the CIA had become concerned that Zia was diverting a large share of the weapons it supplied to the ISI to an extreme Mujahideen group led by Gulbuddin Hekmatyar. Not only was this group anti-American, but its strategy appeared to be aimed at dividing the rest of the Afghan resistance so that it could take over in Kabul—with Zia's support.

Second, there is the Bhutto family. Zia had, after all, usurped power from President Zulfikar Ali Bhutto. He had also allowed Bhutto to be hanged like a common criminal in 1979 on what Bhutto's family viewed as a trumped-up charge. In addition, Zia outlawed Bhutto's political party, the Pakistan People's Party; imprisoned his wife (even though she was suffering from lung cancer) and his daughter, Benazir Bhutto; and had both his sons, who were in exile abroad, convicted of high crimes in absentia. The eldest son, Shah Nawaz, was then murdered in France in 1986, and the younger son, Mir Murtaza, driven into hiding. Demanding vengeance, Mir Murtaza Bhutto headed an anti-Zia group called Al Zulfikar ("the sword"), which operated out of Afghanistan and Syria. One of its operations was to hijack a Pakistan International Airlines Boeing 727 with 100 passengers aboard. Another involved attempting to blow Pak One out of the sky with Zia aboard it by firing a Soviet-built SAM 7 missile at it. In all, Mir Murtaza claimed he was behind five attempts to assassinate Zia. Initially, his group also had taken credit for the successful destruction of Pak One in a phone call to the BBC, but it subsequently retracted this claim. In any case, there was no doubt that he was well motivated. (Mir Murtaza was killed in a shoot out with police in Karachi in 1996.)

A third theory is that the KGB killed Zia. Moscow also had a motive, since Zia was behind covert attacks on Soviet troops not only in Afghanistan but in the Soviet Union itself. Earlier that August, the Soviet Union had temporarily suspended its troop withdrawals from Afghanistan because it alleged that Zia had violated the Geneva Accords, which had been signed in May. A spokesman for the foreign ministry in Moscow said only a week before the crash that Zia's "obstructionist policy cannot be tolerated." Moscow officials even took the extraordinary step of calling in the

American Ambassador to Moscow, Jack Matlock, and informing him that it intended "to teach Zia a lesson." It certainly had the means in place in Pakistan to make this threat credible, having trained, subsidized, and effectively run the Afghan intelligence service, WAD, which operated in Pakistan. In 1988, according to a State Department report, such covert operations had killed and wounded more than 1,400 people in Pakistan.

A fourth theory was that India was the culprit. Less than two weeks before the crash, the Indian prime minister, Rajiv Gandhi, had warned Pakistan that it would have cause "to regret its behavior" in covertly supplying weapons to Sikh terrorists in India. Not only had the Sikhs assassinated Indira Gandhi, Rajiv's mother, when she was prime minister, they now had more than 2,000 armed guerrillas located mainly around the Pakistan border, and Zia had been supplying them with AK-47 assault rifles, rocket launchers, and sanctuaries inside Pakistan. Accordingly, India had a motive to get rid of Zia. It also had the means, having organized a special covert-action unit that went by the initials R.A.W, to recruit agents inside Pakistan.

A fifth theory was that Shiites were behind Zia's death. Zia's Sunni regime had been repressing the Shiite minority, and, according to this theory, the Shiites struck back by recruiting the Shiite copilot of Zia's plane, Wing Commander Sajid. This was why Pakistani military authorities arrested the Shiite pilot of the backup C-130, who was a close friend of Sajid, and interrogated him for more than two months. (Even under torture, he insisted that, as far as he knew, Sajid was a loyal pilot who would not commit suicide.) The problem here was that in order to crash the plane Sajid would have had to overpower the rest of the four-man flight crew, but no such struggle had been heard over the radio.

Finally, there is the Army coup theory. Zia had told his close associates that he planned to purge and reorganize the army, and this threat, according to this theory, would provide a motive for a preemptive move against Zia. Among the few top generals not aboard Pak One was General Aslam Beg, the Army's vice chief of staff. He waved good-bye to Zia from the runway, and then, after the crash, flew immediately to Islamabad to take control, ordering army units to cordon off official residences, government buildings, and other strategic locations in the capital.

My assessment is that Zia and all thirty people aboard Pak One, were victims of sabotage. After going to Islamabad and Lahore to investigate in 1989, I was allowed to read the redcover secret U.S. report on the accident by a U.S. Defense Department official, who asked to remain anonymous. This report reinforced my conclusion that the pilots and flight crew were incapacitated by a quick-acting nerve gas, such as "VX," which is odorless, easily transportable in liquid form, and, when vaporized by a small explosion, would cause paralysis and loss of speech within thirty seconds. VX gas would leave precisely the residue of phosphorous that was found in the chemical analysis of debris from the cockpit. A soda-sized can of VX could have been planted in the air vent of the pilot's compartment and triggered by a pressure sensor to activate on takeoff.

But who did it? All the suspected parties—including Mir Murtazi Bhutto's terrorists—had the capability of obtaining VX or a similar nerve gas, and any of them could have recruited an agent to plant a gas bomb on Pak One, since it had been grounded at the airstrip at Bahawalpur in violation of the prescribed procedure of flying it to the larger airport at Multan, where it could be properly guarded. During its four-hour grounding at Bahawalpur, workers reportedly entered Pak One without being searched in order to work on adjusting its cargo door. One of them could have planted a device. So all the suspects had the means to sabotage the plane. But only one of these parties, the Pakistan military, had the power to stop the planned autopsies, seize the telephone records of calls made to Zia and Rahman just prior to the crash, transfer the military personnel at Bahawalpur who might have witnessed the crime, stifle interrogations of police, and keep the FBI out of the picture. In short, only the Pakistan generals who assumed control that day had the power to create a cover-up that followed the crash. They also had a motive for making it look like something more legitimate than a coup d'état.

In addition, the Pakistan military was the only agency capable of assuring that both President Zia and his second-in-command, General Rahman, were on the plane together. And unless both of these men could be eliminated simultaneously, no regime change could be certain. According to General Rahman's family, whom I interviewed at length in Lahore, General Rahman had not wanted to go to the tank demonstration, but he was told that Zia needed his counsel on an "urgent matter." So, under pressure from a general on Beg's staff, he changed his plans and flew with Zia. But that counsel turned out to be untrue. Not only was Zia surprised to see Rahman on the plane, but, as General Rahman related in a phone call from Bahawalpur to his son just before his death, Zia told him that there was no "urgent matter" requiring his presence on the plane.

Zia's eldest son, Ijaz ul-Haq, also believed that his father had been manipulated by the military into going to the tank demonstration. He told me that his father was in the midst of making major changes in the military hierarchy and saw no point in going to this tank demonstration. He then received "continued calls" from General Mahmud Durrani, who was on Beg's staff, pressing him to be at the demonstration. The general said that the "Americans would consider it a slight" if he missed this event. So, despite his misgivings, he agreed to go. But according to U.S. Ambassador Robert Bigger Oakley, who in August 1988 had been the assistant to the president for Pakistan on the National Security Council, neither the U.S. embassy nor the military mission had pressed for Zia's attendance. He also told me that Ambassador Raphel, his predecessor, made a snap decision twenty-four hours beforehand to fly on Pak One when he learned, to his surprise, that Zia would be aboard the plane. If so, Zia, like Rahman, had been misled by his advisors.

The level of orchestration necessary to bring about this regime change, both before the crash and in effecting the coverup after the crash, persuades me that this was an inside job by a Pakistani military cabal. The journalistic lesson in the Zia case is that even when a government officially embargoes a subject, such as the Pakistan government did in this case, in a relatively porous country such as Pakistan, it is possible to get answers from low-level civil servants, such as air tower controllers, mortuary officers, and police officials.

Chapter 2

THE DEATH OF DAG HAMMARSKJÖLD

In 1961, in the heat of a bloody war of secession in the heart of Africa, UN Secretary General Dag Hammarskjöld tried to mediate between the Republic of the Congo, which had just won its independence from Belgium, and Congo's breakaway mineral-rich province of Katanga, whose self-proclaimed president, Moise Tshombe, and his mercenary forces were secretly financed by the giant mining corporation, Union Minerale. At stake were billions of dollars in annual mineral revenues. To end the conflict, Hammarskjöld arranged a secret meeting in Rhodesia. On September 17, 1961, he took off in a UN-chartered DC-6 airliner from Leopoldville, the capital of the Republic of the Congo, on a 1,000-mile flight to Ndola in Rhodesia. Because of the danger that Union Minerale mercenaries might try to interfere with the mission, a decoy plane was sent ahead and no flight plan was filed. On board, Hammarskjöld was accompanied by only a small staff to maintain secrecy. The captain also maintained radio silence until the plane reached the Rhodesian border at 11:35 p.m. Only then did he notify the control tower at the Ndola airport that the UN plane would land there in less than thirty minutes. This was the last communication with the aircraft. Just after midnight, a large flash of light was seen in the sky near the airport. The next afternoon, the plane's wreckage was found some nine miles from the airport. So were the fifteen badly burned bodies of the members of Hammarskjold's party and the crew. The only survivor was

Hammarskjold's security chief, Harold Julien, who died five days later in a hospital.

Even though the death of the UN Secretary General was no minor matter, investigators could not resolve whether he died by accident or design. The 180-man search party scoured a sixsquare-kilometer area but found few clues. The plane was not equipped with either a black box or cockpit recorder. Swedish, British, and American experts were called in to examine the few pieces of the jigsaw puzzle that were recovered, and they found no signs of structural defects in the plane itself. The altimeters were determined by a U.S. lab to have been in working order at the time of the crash, so there was no technical reason for the pilots to have misjudged their altitude. Nor was there was evidence of fire aboard the plane before the crash. The Rhodesian Board of Investigation ruled the crash a probable accident but said it could not rule out the possibility of sabotage because major parts of the plane were not recovered and several witnesses testified that it had been left unguarded at the Leopoldville airport prior to the flight.

The United Nations then appointed its own Commission of Investigation, but since it relied heavily on the Rhodesian inquiry, its results were also inconclusive. One problem for the UN investigators was that they found out that the corpses of two of Hammarskjöld's Swedish bodyguards had multiple bullet wounds, and bodyguards do not ordinarily get shot in a plane crash. In this case, however, the Rhodesian medical examiners posited that the bullet wounds had been the result of exploding ammunition. The plane did carry ammunition that could have been ignited when the plane burned in the fire after the crash, but ballistics expert Major C. F. Westell found that exploding ammunition would not replicate their actual bullet wounds. He stated, "I can certainly describe as sheer nonsense the

statement that cartridges of machine guns or pistols detonated in a fire can penetrate a human body." Adding further to
the mystery, General Bjorn Egge, who was the first UN official to see Hammarskjöld's body, said in a newspaper interview in 2005 that he had seen a large hole in Hammarskjöld's forehead (and that it had been airbrushed out of the photographs). Since Hammarskjöld was not seated near the ammunition in the rear of the plane, a bullet wound in him would suggest that he had been shot.

Then, in 1998, after the apartheid government fell in South Africa, new evidence emerged from the archives of South Africa's intelligence archive. According to Archbishop Desmond Tutu, the Nobel laureate who headed South Africa's Truth and Reconciliation Commission, documents in the files indicated that a bomb had been planted in the plane's landing gear. One such report implicated both the CIA and Britain's MI-5 in the sabotage, though this could not be verified. The British Foreign Office, in denying its validity, suggested that it may have been planted in the files as disinformation. In any case, without any forensic means of establishing the facts surrounding Hammarskjöld's death, the case could not be settled by a questionable intelligence record. It thus remains an unresolved mystery.

The most innocent theory is that the crash was caused by pilot error. According to it, the pilot, though experienced, was fatigued by the tense flight, and in his approach he misjudged the distance to the airport. A second theory is that the plane was sabotaged by those opposed to Hammarskjöld's efforts to get Tshombe to end the secession of Katanga. There is also a theory that someone aboard the plane tried to hijack it, and a gunfight broke out. This scenario would account for the guards' bullet wounds. Finally, there is the theory that a plane piloted by a mercenary tried to intercept the UN plane after it broke radio silence, and caused the crash. In 2011, A. Susan Williams, a research fellow at the University of London, argued in her book *Who Killed Hammarskjöld?* that there was an explosion before the plane fell from the sky, as the only survivor of the crash, Harold Julien, had testified, and that U.S. intelligence had intercepted a message from the cockpit in which the pilot says "I've hit it."

My assessment is that the crash involved more than pilot error. The problem with both the hijacker and interception theories is that the pilot was in radio contact with the control tower in the last half-hour and, if there had been a battle on the plane or an attack by another aircraft, he certainly would have reported it over the radio or sounded a mayday alert, as he did not suffer bullet wounds. Before the plane was reported missing, several witnesses reported to police a bright flash in the sky. Such an explosion high in the sky could scatter parts of the plane far from where the wreckage was found and account for why they were not found by the search party. Such an explosion would also discount the pilot error theory. So the most compelling explanation is sabotage, possibly an explosive device planted on the plane before it departed and triggered by the lowering of the landing gear. In this scenario, the bullet wounds remain a problem. They could have been the result of a gunman finding the wreckage before the search party and completing the job, or from a guard on the plane discharging his weapon in panic after the explosion. But unless some of the missing pieces of wreckage turn up after a half-century, we will never know the answer.

The lesson here is that an assassination disguised as a plane crash, if not a perfect crime, makes it difficult to definitively identify the culprit by conventional forensic methods. The successful explosion of an aircraft leaves no crime scene and no witnesses.

Chapter 3

KILLING ENRICO MATTEI

Enrico Mattei, an extraordinarily ambitious Italian civil servant, had become by 1962 the arch-nemesis of the international oil cartel. He gained his power in postwar Italy by reorganizing a state entity called Ente Nazionale Idrocarburini, or ENI, which in 1948 had a chain of gas stations and a few natural-gas wells, into a huge conglomerate that supplied most of Italy with its fuel. To feed ENI's refineries in southern Italy, Mattei attempted to make deals in the Middle East that undermined the near-monopoly of the cartel, and its three controlling partners, Exxon (then called Standard Oil of New Jersey), BP (then called Anglo-Iranian Oil), and Royal Dutch Shell. To get a concession in Iran, whose oil up to then went to the cartel for a small royalty, he offered Shah Reza Pahlavi of Iran a much richer cut: a 50-50 partnership on newly discovered oil. The Shah agreed, but ENI failed to find any new oil in Iran. Then, in 1961, at the height of the Cold War, Mattei turned to the only other major source of oil not controlled by the cartel, the Soviet Union. He not only offered to pay them hard currency for its oil but to build a pipeline through Eastern Europe so it could be delivered to Italy. This move was viewed with such deep concern by the new administration of President John F. Kennedy that the administration pressured American companies to cut off the steel exports that Mattei needed for the pipeline. The cartel was also concerned enough to use its leverage over the Italian politicians it was secretly financing, including those in Italy's ruling Christian Democracy Party, to get the government to derail the Soviet oil agreement. After Exxon offered to supply ENI with Libyan oil on condition that it terminate the deal, Mattei asked for a personal meeting with President Kennedy. It was scheduled for November 1962. But on October 27 of that year, at a critical point in Mattei's negotiations with both the Soviet Union and the United States, he was killed when his company plane crashed in Northern Italy.
The circumstances of the crash were as follows: The Morane-Saulnier MS-760 plane had taken off from Catania, Sicily, around midday en route to Milan. Only three people were aboard the small jet: Mattei; the pilot Irnerio Bertuzzi; and William McHale, an American reporter who was interviewing Mattei. All three men died when the plane fell from the sky and crashed in a blazing fire near the village of Bascape.
The official inquiry was headed by Giulio Andreotti, the defense minister and political strongman of the Christian Democracy party. In 1962, the forensics for determining the cause of air crashes was heavily dependent on recovering the plane's flight instruments, as there were no black boxes or flight recorders on small planes. In this case, however, key pieces of the plane's instruments had been inexplicably destroyed at the scene. The flight gauges, for example, had been dissolved in acid. So, without any direct evidence of an explosion, the investigation was stymied. After determining from weather reports that there had been thunderstorms in the area, it was ruled that the crash a "probable accident" caused by bad weather.
Even with this official finding, there was considerable suspicion in Italy that more was involved than a thunderstorm, and the Mattei crash became the subject of countless journalistic investigations. In 1995, the remains of Mattei and his pilot were exhumed by court order and reexamined by a panel of experts. Even though thirty-three years had

elapsed, there were now more accurate forensic tools. And through them, the panel found tiny bits of metal in the crash victims' bones. They further determined that these fragments had been deformed by an enormous pressure before the fiery crash, and they concluded that there was an explosion inside the plane. This new analysis suggested that Mattei had been the victim of an assassination. In light of the international intrigue surrounding Mattei at the time of his death, numerous conspiracy theories have been advanced as to who was behind the assassination. To begin with, there is the contract-killing theory. According to Tomasso Buscetti, an ex-Mafia "pentito" who also provided leads in the Roberto Calvi case, the Sicilian Mafia was given the contract to kill Mattei on behalf of American oil interests and had one of its men put a bomb aboard the plane in Catania. Even though Buscetti's allegation was unsubstantiated, it led to the 1995 exhumation of the bodies. (Buscetti claimed that the Andreotti investigation was merely a cover-up.) Next, there is a "French Connection" theory. According to Philippe Thyraud de Vosjoli, a former agent of the French secret service SDECE, Mattei's plane was sabotaged by a SDECE operative code-named Laurent, who placed high explosives on board that would be triggered by its landing gear. And finally, the CIA theory: that CIA operatives sabotaged Mattei's plane to prevent him from building the pipeline to the Soviet Union.

The fact that a small plane crashed in 1962 in bad weather is not in itself suspicious, but if there was an explosive device aboard it, there can be little doubt that Mattei was murdered. My assessment is that this was the work of an intelligence service. In an exhaustive review of the forensic evidence in 2009, Italian academics Donato Firrao and Graziano Ubertalli concluded that "a small charge bomb had been planted behind the dashboard from the exterior of the plane." This job was most likely done by the agent of an experienced intelligence service. In this context, I find the account of Philippe De Vosjoli credible. I spent two days interviewing de Vosjoli in Lighthouse Point, Florida, in 1980, and I believe he was in a position to know about SDECE's covert operations. He recalled that French intelligence had mounted a similar attack on March 29, 1959, on a plane carrying Barthélemy Boganda, the prime minister of a French territory that is now the Central African Republic. Boganda's plane exploded in midair about 100 miles west of the airport at Bangui. According to de Vosjoli, a miniature explosive was used by French intelligence operatives to make the assassination appear to be an accident. De Vosjoli said the same technique was repeated by French intelligence in 1962 to eliminate Mattei. Even though de Vosjoli had no evidence to back his theory, his description of the explosive device is consistent with the findings of the 1997 forensic analysis and, in my view, gives further weight to his story that French intelligence had a hand in the downing of Mattei's aircraft.

In 1962, before forensic investigative techniques for determining the cause of plane crashes had been fully perfected, the theory that Mattei's plane crashed because of bad weather was perfectly plausible. In 1995, more highly developed forensics changed the scientific verdict from a likely accident to a likely murder.

Chapter 4

VANISHING LIN BIAO

In the fall of 1971, Marshal Lin Biao, the designated successor of Mao Zedong to rule China, suddenly disappeared from view. The annual National Day celebration, in which he was expected to appear on the podium in his customary place next to Mao, and which had been held every year since the Communists took power in 1948, was abruptly cancelled, and Lin Biao was not mentioned in any newspaper or television broadcast for nearly two years. During this period, only the top leadership learned that he was dead. Mao explained that Marshal Lin, who had been his comrade-in-arms and Communist China's most decorated hero, was a traitor who had been planning to assassinate him and then stage a coup d'état that September. After the putative plot was uncovered, Mao had the entire military command secretly purged and ordered Lin arrested. According to Mao, Lin then attempted to defect to the Soviet Union, which was now China's enemy, but his military aircraft ran out of fuel and crashed in Mongolia, killing Lin Biao and all aboard the fleeing plane. So, in this official account, released to the public in 1973, Lin died in an accidental plane crash.

The basic facts emerged only gradually. On September 13, 1971, a British-made Trident airliner, powered by three jet engines, took off from Shanhaiguan Airbase in eastern China, flew less than 1,000 miles into Mongolia, a vassal state of the Soviet Union, and then crashed into the grasslands near the town of Ondorkhaan. Aboard the doomed aircraft were Lin Biao, his entire family, and a half-dozen of his top aides. No one survived the crash. The weather was clear that day, the plane was well within its range of 2,000 miles at the time of the crash, and the officer at the plane's controls, Colonel Pan Jungyin, who was a deputy commander of the Chinese air force, was one of China's most experienced pilots.

Mongolia, which was not an ally of China's in 1971, conducted only a perfunctory investigation. It established that the plane had not run out of fuel. Indeed, there was so much excess fuel in the pods that it fed a blazing fire that incinerated most of the plane, including all of its flight instruments. No autopsies were conducted on the badly charred bodies, which were buried in a shallow mass grave near the crash site. Because the plane was well beyond the range of China's primitive surface-to-air missiles, the investigators ruled out the possibility that the aircraft had been downed by a Chinese missile. And as there was no other aircraft detected in this area, they concluded that the crash was an accident caused by pilot error.

Moscow, apparently not satisfied that it was an accident, subsequently sent in a KGB team to exhume the remains. The results of this investigation were kept secret but, according to a KGB defector who claimed that he had had access to the investigation, Soviet pathologists determined that some of the passengers aboard the plane died before it crashed and burned.

U.S. intelligence was also suspicious of the circumstances surrounding the crash. The NSA was closely monitoring communication, radar, and other signals in China as part of the preparations for President Richard Nixon's trip to China. Through its signals intercepts on September 13, 1971, it learned that China had grounded all military plane flights just before Lin's flight took off and that the flights only resumed after his plane crashed. This extraordinary shutdown suggests that a decision was made by Mao to allow the flight. At no point did Mao seem concerned that the plane would make it to the Soviet Union. When Mao was told by his premier Chou En-Lai that Lin's plane was about to take off, he calmly recited to Chou an ancient Chinese proverb that began "Rain must fall." According to Dr. Li Zhisui, Mao's personal physician, who wrote his memoirs after he emigrated to the United States, after the plane crashed Mao was greatly relieved to hear that there were no survivors. But if Mao wanted Lin Biao dead, could he have depended on a random accident to bring about this outcome? All that is known for certain is that the counter-coup that Mao feared never took place.

The vacuum left by the suppression of virtually all the evidence concerning the crash has been filled by numerous theories. Even the official finding that the crash was caused by pilot error is no more than a theory. An alternative theory is that the plane was sabotaged. According to this theory, Lin Biao was encouraged to leave China with his wife, son, and military aides, but a time or pressure-activated bomb was planted aboard their plane. There is also the staged crash theory advanced by Stanislav Lunev, who had served as a high-ranking intelligence officer on the Russian General Staff. According to Lunev, Lin Biao and his party had been executed and their corpses then placed on the plane and that after flying the corpse-filled aircraft towards the Mongolian border, the Chinese pilot set the controls on auto-pilot, and parachuted out. Lunev does not explain what purpose would be served by such an elaborate staging of an accident.

My assessment is that Lin Biao's jet did not accidently fall from the sky. The weather was clear, the plane was at its cruising altitude, there was no evidence of a fuel shortage, and there were no distress calls. A more plausible explanation is that Mao had intervened to make certain that Marshal Lin never reached Moscow alive, and that a timed explosive had been planted aboard the plane. This bomb would account for why the plane was allowed to take off, why Chinese fighters did not attempt to intercept it, and why Mao told Chou that "The rain must fall." Quite possibly, the explosion was planned to occur over Chinese territory, where the cover-up could be managed, but because of the lack of headwinds, the plane made it to Mongolia. In any case, I believe that the plane crashed because of Chinese sabotage.

The obvious lesson here is that a regime in a closed society can control the shape and timing of the information about a crime. Even though the information in this case concerned a political leader as prominent as Marshal Lin Biao, the regime managed to suppress any mention of it in public for two years. To be sure, this crime occurred more than four decades ago, but the regime in China still retains that same power over information, as is illustrated by the murder of Neil Heywood in Chongqing, China, on November 14, 2011. Heywood, who was a British consultant to Bo Xilai, then a powerful member of the China's ruling politburo, was found dead in his hotel room. His death was officially attributed to his alcohol consumption, even though a secret police report showed that he had been poisoned by potassium cyanide. His body was cremated before an autopsy could be performed. The natural-death verdict went unchallenged for three months, and it would have remained largely forgotten if not for the defection of Wang Lijun, the local police chief and vice-mayor, to the U.S. Embassy in February 2012. After Wang revealed that Heywood was murdered by Gu Kailai, the wife of Bo Xilai, the Chinese regime decided to reveal the murder. It purged Bo Xilai, and, after extracting a confession from Gu, convicted her of the murder. Yet it still controlled all the evidence, and it may have used the portions of it that it elected to release, as it did in the Lin Bia case, to justify political changes.

APPENDIX A

POLITICAL PLANE CRASHES

DATE	LOCATION	VICTIM
SEPTEMBER 7, 1940	Paraguay	Paraguayan dictator President José Félix Estigarribia
JULY 4, 1943	Gibraltar	Polish resistance leader Władysław Sikorski
MARCH 17, 1957	Cebu, Philippines	Philippines President Ramon Magsaysay
SEPTEMBER 18, 1957	Zambia	UN Secretary General Dag Hammarskjöld
APRIL 13, 1966	Iraq	Iraqi President Abdul Salam Arif
APRIL 27, 1969	Mongolia	Chinese Vice Premier Lin Biao
DECEMBER 4, 1980	Portugal	Portuguese Prime Minister Francisco de Sá Carne
MAY 24, 1981	Ecuador	Ecuadorian President Jaime Roldós Aguilera
JULY 31, 1981	Panama	Panamanian dictator Omar Torrijos
OCTOBER 19, 1986	Mozambique	Mozambique president Samora Machel
AUGUST 17, 1988	Pakistan	Pakistani President Zia ul-haq
APRIL 6, 1994	Rwanda	Rwanda president Juvénal Habyarimana and Burunda president Cyprien Ntaryamira
FEBRUARY 26, 2004	Bosnia	Macadonia President Boris Trajkovski
OCTOBER 19, 2006	Nigeria	Sultan of Sokoto, head of Nigerian Supreme Council for Islamic Affairs
APRIL 10, 2010	Russia	Polish President Lech Kaczyn'ski

About The Author

Edward Jay Epstein was born on December 6, 1935 in Brooklyn, New York. He attended Cornell University where he received a Master degree (Government) and Harvard University, where he received a PhD (Government). He taught political science at MIT and was the Regent Professor, American Government, at UCLA. He was a staff writer for the New Yorker, and columnist for *Manhattan, Inc* and *Slate*. He is the author of 15 books, eight of which have been excerpted in the *New Yorker, Atlantic* and *Sunday Times of London*. His master's thesis on the search for political truth became the best-selling book *Inquest: The Warren Commission and the Establishment of Truth*. His doctoral dissertation on television news was published as News From Nowhere. He is the recipient of numerous foundation grants and awards, including the prestigious Financial Times/ Booz Allen prize for both best biography and best business book for his book *Dossier: The Secret History of Armand Hammer*. He resides in New York City.

The Series EDWARD JAY EPSTEIN INVESTIGATES

Volume I   Why Political Inquests Fail
Volume II   Assassinations in the Sky
Volume III Political Assassinations
Volume IV   Suicides and Disguised Murders
Volume V   Suspicious Endings

Printed in Great Britain
by Amazon